REA

ACPL ‖‖‖‖‖‖‖‖‖‖‖‖‖‖‖‖‖‖‖‖‖
3 1833 0273   Y0-ABQ-039
894.
DISCARDED
Orbán, Otto.
The blood of the Walsungs

'S

ALLEN COUNTY PUBLIC LIBRARY
FORT WAYNE, INDIANA 46802

You may return this book to any location of
the Allen County Public Library.

DEMCO

OTTÓ ORBÁN
(PHOTO: LÁSZLÓ CSIGÓ)

OTTÓ ORBÁN
The Blood
of the Walsungs
SELECTED POEMS

EDITED BY
George Szirtes

CORVINA

BLOODAXE BOOKS

Allen County Public Library
900 Webster Street
PO Box 2270
Fort Wayne, IN 46801-2270

Copyright © Ottó Orbán
1965, 1970, 1973, 1976, 1978, 1981, 1984, 1987, 1990, 1992, 1993.
Translations copyright © George Szirtes, László T. András, László Baránszky, John Bátki, Alan Dixon, Gerard Gorman, Jascha Kessler, Maria Körösy, Nicholas Kolumbán, Edwin Morgan, Eric Mottram, Marc Nasdor, William Jay Smith, Timea K. Szell, 1993.

ISBN: 1 85224 203 5   Bloodaxe Books
       963 13 3840 1   Corvina Books

First published 1993 by
Bloodaxe Books Ltd,
P.O. Box 1SN,
Newcastle upon Tyne NE99 1SN.

Published in Hungary by
Corvina Books,
Vörösmarty tér 1,
Budapest 1051.

Bloodaxe Books Ltd acknowledges
the financial assistance of Northern Arts.

ACKNOWLEDGEMENTS
Acknowledgements are due to the Arts Council
for providing a translation grant for this book.

LEGAL NOTICE
All rights reserved. No part of this book may be
reproduced, stored in a retrieval system, or
transmitted in any form, or by any means, electronic,
mechanical, photocopying, recording or otherwise,
without prior written permission from Bloodaxe Books Ltd.
Requests to publish work from this book
must be sent to Bloodaxe Books Ltd.

Cover printing by J. Thomson Colour Printers Ltd, Glasgow.

Printed in Great Britain by
Cromwell Press Limited,
Broughton Gifford, Melksham, Wiltshire.

Books of poetry by Ottó Orbán

1 *Fekete Ünnep* (Black Feast) 1960
2 *A teremtés napja* (The Day of Creation) 1963
3 *Búcsú Bethlehemtől* (Goodbye to Bethlehem) 1965
4 *A föltámadás elmarad* (The Resurrection is Postponed) 1970
5 *Emberáldozat* (Human Sacrifice) 1973
6 *Távlat a történethez* (Perspective for the Story) 1976
7 *A visszacsavart láng* (The Flame turned Down) 1978
8 *Az alvó vulkán* (The Dormant Volcano) 1981
9 *Szép nyári nap, a párkák szótlanul figyelnek*
   (A Fine Summer Day, the Parcae Silently Watching) 1984
10 *A mesterségről* (On Technique) 1984
11 Collected Poems 1986
12 *A fényes cáfolat* (The Brilliant Refutation) 1987
13 *A kozmikus gavallér* (The Cosmic Cavalier) 1990
14 *Egyik oldaláról a másikra fordul; él*
   (He turns from One side to the Other; He's Alive) 1992
15 *A keljföljancsi jegyese* (The Self-righting Doll's Betrothed) 1992

The numbers above correspond to the numbers printed after the titles of poems
in the Contents list opposite.

Translators

GS	George Szirtes
LTA/WJS	László T. András and William Jay Smith
LB/MN	László Baránszky and Marc Nasdor
JB	John Bátki
AD	Alan Dixon
GG	Gerard Gorman
JK	Jascha Kessler
JK/MK	Jascha Kessler and Maria Körösy
NK	Nicholas Kolumbán
EGM	Edwin Morgan
EM	Eric Mottram
TKS	Timea K. Szell

Contents

3. A VISIT TO ROOM 104

Introduction

The poems of Ottó Orbán are instantly recognisable to a Hungarian reader: marked by a brisk, vernacular, apparently unliterary, unconfined energy, they carry an authority blended of the humorous and tragic, of the commonplace and extraordinary. Often they take the form of anecdote or comment. A voice buttonholes the reader, carries him along in its narrative sweep, then detonates a mine (or several mines) under his feet before returning to the texture of dialogue. The voice appears almost garrulous at first, afflatus and deflation quickly succeeding each other, seemingly engaged in some violent internal argument. The whole procedure seems to have a dizzy, scat quality about it which spins free of formal constraint.

Having been the translator of Allen Ginsberg's 'Howl' it isn't surprising that Orbán was for a while regarded as Hungary's own beat poet. This opinion had a pinch of truth in it but it was far from the whole truth: Orbán in his long career has also translated Chaucer, Auden, Dylan Thomas and Robert Lowell among many others, and is an acknowledged master-craftsman. His own poems too, on careful listening, are revealed to be highly disciplined. Under the unliterary tone lies a deep literary sophistication, a craftsmanship that diverts attention from itself to its subject matter. The field of reference is wide and rich, ghosts of English iambics and Latin hexameters hover about the verse. The mines however are real, and it is only Orbán's literary self-discipline and humanity that prevents them from blowing the poems up.

The texture of the dialogue is therefore vital: it is what most accurately defines him. This texture, as with most poets, is derived from the formative experiences of his life. If the inner argument is violent it is because life is perceived to be so. As he says in one of his later confessional "sonnets":

> I'm of that parting generation whose baptism of fire
> bequeathed them epilepsy and a sense of solid values.
> The moderns in their screaming nosedive showered us
> with cream-puffs that exploded. I tasted them
> and have been this way since, standing by the cellar,
> light, light, infinite light and a fluttering, the wrecked yard.

The baptism of fire and the wrecked yard belong to the war, but so does that 'sense of solid values' alternating with epilepsy. As an eight year old child in 1945 Orbán was living in central Budapest, close to the river. He was the product of a mixed marriage, a Jewish father and Christian mother, both solidly middle-class, but rather on the slide since 1938 because of anti-semitic laws. The family had had an opportunity to emigrate to Argentina but a sense of obligation kept them in Hungary. The tenement block into which they had moved when Ottó was two years old was a social microcosm within which they found a respectable enough place and where life proceeded with a degree of regularity, or at least a show of comfort circumscribed only by increasing poverty. Then the air-raids started. Orbán vividly describes the braying of the sirens in one of his essays: it was a constant feature of his childhood. The Germans arrived in the spring of 1944. His father disappeared into a prison camp, the nearby bridge was blown up. Saturation bombing begot a cellar-based existence where each excursion into the daylit world became an exercise in surrealism. A woman on the third floor, a solicitor's wife, insisting on her daily bath took up a basin full of water from the yard. After a particularly severe raid in which nearby houses were brought down she returned to her bathroom to find an unexploded bomb. She screamed out in her terror, 'There's a bomb sitting in my tub!' The macabre and comic image of the sitting bomb provides an early key to the young Ottó's imagination.

The beginnings of his career as a writer are just as unusual. A bright, artistically-gifted child, his ability was quickly recognised by his middle-brow family. But in the spring of 1945 he learned that his father had died and that, being fatherless, he would be sent to live in an institute along with others in his position. In the meantime his mother took up with someone else and a half-brother was the result. The young talent of the family circle now became the prodigy of the institute. One of the teachers encouraged the traumatised children in her charge to write poems as a form of therapy. Within a short time some of them had managed to shape their experiences into poetry which was soon published and widely circulated. This was not the last time Orbán was to discover the therapeutic value of writing poetry. Part of the therapy lay in success. While still at the institute he was asked to edit an anthology of children's war poetry, was interviewed on radio and received by the Minister for Information. The success surprised his family and slightly frightened them. The prodigy had become public property: it appeared to Orbán's mother that she had lost not only her husband but her son too. Orbán himself does not have a particularly high regard for his poems of that period: he does not include any in his collected poems, though he does quote a pair of lines in an autobiographical essay. Inadvertently he had created an expectancy and an audience without quite knowing what poetry was. He was, in his own words, 'an ordinary, scruffy, neanderthal child' with a pleasant sense of his own importance.

Since 1947 he had been making frequent visits home and there met the various men in his mother's life. One of these eventually married her. The early fifties closed about Hungarian society. A woman in the Orbán's block who was officially regarded as a 'class alien' turned to drink and threw up in the lift. A notice appeared there the next day saying: 'Whoever is sick in the lift is an enemy of the people'. The tenement block saw considerable movement: class enemies were exiled to the country and new lodgers were settled in. In the meantime, unlike his half-brother, Orbán was enjoying considerable academic success. Comparisons inevitably caused friction at home.

He was seventeen and still at grammar school when he discovered the poetry of Dezső Kosztolányi, and became intoxicated by its music. Having grown accustomed to producing 'free verse' based entirely on content he was suddenly seized by the delights of pure form. His first attempts at it were disastrous, and one of his teachers, the outstanding, but at that time still banned, poet Ágnes Nemes Nagy, told him as much. Nevertheless, within six months he had written the poem with which his collected poems were later to open: his subject, the war. Rimbaud lurks in the background, the ghosts of *Le Bateau Ivre* lurch through Orbán's own quatrains. He was still naive. As he was later to say, he had written poems but was not yet a poet. Despite his prizes and commendations, the university refused Orbán's application. His stepfather objected to his further attempts to enrol, and even more vigorously to his poetry. Eventually he was thrown out and resorted to sleeping on benches or at friends' flats. At the same time he received his first official translating commission. By 1956 he had been taken on at the university, and could return home to live. Then came the doomed uprising which marked a rapprochement between Orbán and his mother. His half-brother emigrated after the defeat of the revolution. Orbán himself was not an actor in the events, merely a witness. In 1957 he broke down from nervous exhaustion. Soon after his recovery he married and became a father. His mother was shortly to die of a brain tumour.

Such potted lives inevitably leave out the present and the immediate past but sometimes they may serve to annotate one or other tendency in a writer's work. The breakdown interrupted Orbán's education but also saw the publication of his first volume of verses. The immediate result of this was that Orbán moved from *wunderkind* to *enfant terrible* in critical opinion. Some time later, in reviewing his 1972 volume, *Emberáldozat* (Human Sacrifice) the critic Balázs Lengyel was quick to point out – lest the reader should imagine Orbán to be gripped by some sort of terminal infantilism – that the poet had grown up, and that he had done so within the framework of confessional verse. Lengyel suggests that the young Orbán was attempting a synthesis of Pilinszky and Ginsberg, a suggestion which Orbán himself confirms, in one of his later poems, 'Egyéniség' ('Individualism', included in this selection). But Dylan Thomas, García Lorca and Attila József were also early influences. The poets commonly referred to as confessional, such as Robert Lowell, came later.

War has been an abiding theme for Orbán: whatever the subject he demands it be tested in the crucible of his wartime experience. As he has become a much travelled writer, the encounter with other cultures has become more important, as has the question of art itself, particularly the conflict between the beatific and the terrible. The visionary element reappears with great regularity in his work. He begins his poem, 'The Apparition' with an assertion:

> Yes, an angel has summoned me too.
> though not just like Blake or Weöres:
> kindling a freemasonic burning bush in my room
> or dictating lines to me over the phone...

The continuation defines his own spiritus mundi:

> 'Come on,' the voice said, 'there's no one at home.'
> The shoddy victory among ancient furniture
> was outlined sharply in the cigarette-smoke:
> there we lay on the World War I family bed,
> like monumental sculptures bathed in sweat.

And ends with a typical defiant rhetorical gesture.

> 'O shaggy mustang, O fiery youth!'
> plunging in Professor Piccard's live bathyscaphe
> into the abyssal wheezing I again fell asleep.

Formally, he is extremely versatile, and has written with some virtuosity in a variety of styles, but arguably his greatest achievements have been within the realms of the prose poem and the fourteen-line unrhymed, often dactylic, "sonnet", in which he freely admits his debt to Lowell and to a lesser extent Berryman

14

though the reference to 'Mr Bones' derives not from him but from Marcel Aymé's *Le passe-muraille* – and from the poet's own illness. These two forms have persisted through his work over many years. The prose poems came first, the earliest appearing in 1961, but he has continued writing them into the present day. The sonnets begin some twenty years later but in recent years have been taking over from the prose poems, as a form of spiritual diary. These work through the ghosts of classical metre and seem to be capable of infinite extension. It is in these that Orbán has become the leading commentator on the politics and social life of his times. Berryman and Lowell put the form to the same kind of use but Orbán never really sounds like any other poet: he is always precisely himself, mannerisms, mines and all. The idiom he speaks is characteristic of Budapest. The ironies are close in tone to the notorious black jokes of the fifties. If Orbán brings a current British poet to mind at all it is Peter Porter. There is a likeness in the apparent garrulousness, in the range of reference, even in the ironic yet questing attitude to experience.

The *enfant terrible* is not totally buried. He is the one who lays the mines in the busy streets of Orbán's verse, the one whom the older poet looks back to and trusts. Now in his fifties, and subject to attacks of a debilitating disease, Orbán's work has gathered a devil-may-care air of freedom. Paradoxically the poems have grown graver and more human.

Despite the earlier avowals of poetry as therapy there is another process described by Orbán in one of his marvellous prose poems, 'A Small Country 1':

> I don't believe that poetry is a care package dropped from a helicopter among those in a bad way. The poem, like a bloodhound, is driven by its instincts after the wounded prey. But the latter will change form and essence on the run… It cajoles, with a reasonable image of the future, a passion for gambling.

It is the gambling, and not the care package, which invests his own poetry with danger, humanity and his own inimitably grim high-spirits.

GEORGE SZIRTES

1. Report on the Poem

Poets

They stand in the gateway of the century the haunters of the future
with their naïve intelligentsia ideas about beauty and society
in stiff collars walking stick in hand
carving original naturalness into fatal postures
their instincts undermining the postures
in a dying world where no more credit is given to academic death-tolls
to a tearful bluffing and enchanting elegisings about a fleeting mood
they are the credulous dancers at Time's carnival
the lions of this chandeliered ballroom where always
perfume mingled with gunsmoke
real sorrow with sham
and simple courage drowned in a flood of heroic appearances
they invented new notions ideals and points of reference
as well as new anxieties and disgraces
masters and dupes of the modern
they are the ones pathetic and admirable
who went to Spain China Russia Japan
to wink back at History's concubine and extend a hand to mankind
here where a lesser Orpheus wrote cheap verses on dizzying vistas
where a bearded madman sang the praises of violence in Biblical tones
shadows and roses
where a Latin adventurer flashed like a bull's forehead
where the good and the bad both hugged the ground in terror of the
    sky
in the company of goatherds and farm labourers who didn't give a
    damn about poetry
where they discovered love and exploitation
they are the witnesses that man was not meant for death
his ashes are consumed by grass
but his bones stick up from the earth like swords.

[WJS/LTA]

18

Gaiety and Good Heart

On this heavenly molehill
where a long-drawn-out war is being waged besides the local massacres
and the anonymous heroes of time squatting in the dug-outs of their days
know that a smile is only self-deception and joy is death's moratorium
for major causes are composed of minor causes
for victory is unreal in a battle where
peasants' huts are bombed with figures
for the business of living is a master sculptor and can twist a man's face
      to a sheep's
and in hunger there is neither poetry nor sense of the fundamentals
on this earth where poverty is no news
and no one is fool enough to stammer or cry in deep emotion
for who has not clambered down from some cross or other
and who has not soaked his nail-stuck feet in a bowl of water
what typist has not sprung to life again after her family was sent to the ovens
and who has not forgotten her unforgettable lover's features
where everybody but everybody has shaken hands with the bereaved widow
assuring her of his sympathy gazing deep into her eyes
and has cabled ALL THE BEST on hearing of the resurrection of
      Lazarus
where the idea of endurance was invented to meet the torture-chamber
where there is no one who has not seen it all
and who does not have endless opportunities
and who would gladly not exchange state affairs for a fishing-rod
on the breast of this barren mother
when the stars of cosmic paralysis transfix you to the dust
and you lean on the rail and look down into the valley
you can see the hope of the age the little rickety truck
stuffed with whatever has been salvaged from the fire
sticks of furniture sacks stewpans chickens
like an unkillable bombardier-beetle
like a tin-jowled reptile flashing headlamp-eyes
and lolling out its panting petrol-tongue like a child
while in front of the flames embossed on its jolting flanks
the nickel trade-mark shines:
Gaiety and Good Heart

[EGM]

Report on the Poem

From now on, the Earth. Prose of Earth's gravity. Ferroconcrete sea.
Pro boxer grows old. Passions too raw for poetry
in the empty harbor, where no one wipes off tears:
   'It's time!' It is too, and the decent poet

inscribes on wood-free paper: 'Age of Manhood,'
and noble emotion and restrained tears shake in his voice,
like a condom thrown in a puddle. Enough of that.
   It's the old girl's cosmetics that bore me. Let her

tame panthers on her cloudlike walks or wag her hips
in angel-feathers under the stagy moon. She can hold out
her tricksy salvation, thick arias for thickheads: I know what it's
     worth.
   From now on, the story is more important.

The It-Happens-To-Us-All. The Only-To-Me. The Don't-Turn-
     Back.
The fact that won't be changed by star-soaring composition.
The fate that from unseen motives aims at a single goal
   may be smalltime, yet a matter of life and death.

From now on, the logistics-poetry of polar exploration. Foxhole
     letters.
In place of magic eye-and-ear enchantment: stout boots, warm clothes.
Head-clutching verse, a circus stunt,
   flight of fancy with head-in-sand.

That's how it is. Sad that our concepts of God are always man-faced.
Better to fly on wings of pity, but the interrogator comes from the
     interrogated.
To smoke cigarettes with spine-sized tobacco-stalks to ashes,
   anger and love, give me a light!

[EGM]

The Apparition

Yes, an angel has summoned me too,
though not just like Blake or Weöres:
kindling a freemasonic burning bush in my room
or dictating lines to me over the phone.
'Come on,' the voice said, 'there's no one at home.'
The shoddy victory among the ancient furniture
was outlined sharply in the cigarette-smoke:
there we lay on the World War I family bed,
like monumental sculptures bathed in sweat.
My mouth was chapped, wine
after vodka isn't good.

The apparition kept me waiting till morning.

The wizened face and the black hair-tangles –
that's what I saw. Enough
for some nameless secret distress
opening lashless eyes in my cells
to sense the ray-scarred huntsman camouflaging his trap.
Not that I can say he told me anything,
in advance, I mean, the metaphysical messenger.
The hospital, the dying, the 'Daddy Orbán,'
the pedestrian Odyssey from shilling to shilling,
the holed socks, the outgrown shoes, the 'Who's going to say hello?',
in a word the whole piss-and blood-smelling novel
which Central Europe works up
from the Verona balcony-scene,
and even the guerrilla raids of more universal bad luck,
the biological mines, planted in the loam of pleasure,
detonating and detonating
in heart and stomach – all that remained hidden.
Only – the curtain went up on an ancient puppet-show,
and around us so-called destiny:
a theatrical Danube, shores scarred by industry,
a Tom Thumb country with the stolidity of a giant
darkening the sky with smoke and poverty.
How should I know whether fire scared me or deadly cold?
In some murderous medium, flashing up and down,
the butterfly-creature was in terror;

no doubt about it, already drawn to the lamp
men usually call: love.

I smoked a cigarette: modern film-hero.

But later, as the siege and the orphanage
only made a little savage of me, yet not so humourless
as to pluck a verse-harp at that crucial moment:
'O shaggy mustang, O fiery youth!'
plunging in Professor Piccard's live bathyscaphe
into the abyssal wheezing I again fell asleep.

[EGM]

The Ladies of Bygone Days

Where with their magnetic breasts are Susanna and Martha
    and the Judys of various addresses
time has chewed to pulp Melinda and Vera and Liz my god we had
    breakfast with her bacon and eggs
Gisella what on earth was her last name gone too gone off on a Danube
    steamer
all I know about her is she was a company typist somewhere and she
    never heard of contraception till I told her and
then it was all amazement under blonde eyebrows and her Iseult-type
    blue headlights lit up
and I remember Eva too and her caveman-girlfriend the sculptress
    with her low forehead
and the gold-brown madness that looked for lasting messages among
    the trembly lacework revives
its search in their Indian laps for New World treasures
    and the Copernican theory of their hips
over the Babylonian blind the legend ALBERT HECKLER MEN'S
    TAILOR sings out and our tongues incur damnation by the urgency
    of one unpostponable kiss
and what's Tonia that wild spinster doing in Paris and where are
    the adventuresses those Aggies and Cathys and Andreas taking buses
    to with their bursting shopping-bags
they have split dispersed gone without a message all over the stubble-
    field of civilisation
it makes no odds who did what the spicy details for instance whose
    husband it was dropped drunk from a New York taxi
they all live somewhere on the earth live well live poor no need to
    worry energy is conserved
where last year's snow was there's a green of this year's spring
dynasty marked for downfall youth crowned with arrogance the jacket
    taken out of pawn fitted your royal figure like a glove
ah spirit of heartrending elegies turn your noble eyes to Kertész Street
peeling plaster and whores and pensioners brought down in the world
G.T. the poet reeking of suntan-oil sported a newspaper in his breast-
    pocket for use as a flying carpet if the right moment came
and two true lovers merged into one body under a world-broad crackle
    of paper
while on the table Miguel Hernández was dying in a gaol of laurel-
    scented terza rimas

and his flashing bones made lightning in the room and lit up the
    legend tacked to the wall A FRIEND'S FLAT IS NO BROTHEL
and apocalyptic whimpers stole out from the freedom-flavoured stench
on the undying day of the faceless watches when language had still
    to invent the future tense
where the mother of two tempered by shivering fever-fits with a jug
    of milk in her hand cycles smash into a lorry
and the three-dimension-clasping limbs are crushed flat into the sheet
    of an asphalt-album scrawled with skid-marks
in happy mother's present time the green blades of the earth besieged
    the world's ice
and the scarlet of Viking lips swam on the shoreless sea of a cushion
and the bodiless starpelt panther lolled and clanked in its planet-kennel
    retracting its workaday claws
Downy creatures dusty earth-chicks your firm flesh and your elegance
the tongues chirping with 'I says' and 'I don't want none'
but I plan to live forever on a dilapidated iron bed admiring the
    expertise of your professor fingers
with you away sky and memory shiver shudder bleak
but strolling the world on the leash of your arms among the machine-
    gunpitted walls was wonderful
wrinkling at the grave my nose picked up immortal scent from the
    embers of your bodies
I watched my enchanted ones grunt over the mud of bombs in the
    besieged sty
and the wartime Circe had neither chiton nor curls of a goddess
    and Greek urn-figures were not her style
nothing is more perilously beautiful than the live mines of your laps
the history of your hair whispers pleasure in this bomb-crater rolling
    round the sun
the spinning wheel of fate has threaded your arms about my vertebrae
    for good
to step from the burning bush of your slips you mutter to me and it's
    hoarse GIVE ME A LIGHT
while our shivering cells devour each other in a sweat of honey
and embers of spring of creation-the-destroyer hiss through our fingers.

[EGM]

24

Canto

I had wanted for years to translate Pound
  not that I felt close to him far from it
I was intrigued by the puzzle of personality
  Wit and Violence
which is the position of the intellectual in this century
  where the classical serum has proved ineffective against the viruses
    of damnation
and of course the poetic balloon could have done well for a weight
  with the hidden medium of this spiritual conjuration: America
its scandalous vistas strain the eye enough to call up the infinite
  the mirror on which tact can't smear to a blur
the depressing ghost story of reality
  as it does in the elastic memory of countries inured to defeat
THE POET IN THE CAGE is a parable and test
  even allowing for the bankers' revenge
We must decide which way our sympathies should go
  to the wild beast locked in the cage who teaches art to the black
    NCO
or to the NCO who speaks the 'ain't no nothing' language
  but carves a table for the shivering old man
Clearly all this is the basis of a new poetics
  unity of place and time in the age-long emergency
the what-how-and-when and chiefly the what-never-at-any-cost
  clashing in occasional dialectics
for what does it matter if one is not wicked oneself
  but smells the stench of carcasses as though it were the fragrance
    of violets
My disappointment in the text then grew deeper and deeper
  nowhere the key a reference an explanation
unless the swooning snobbery of the nouveau riche is taken for that
  The verse overflowed with Florence the chronicles and Messrs
    So-and-So
and any number of Chinese sages
  Tradition as art relic leaves me cold
in the outskirts where as a boy I was often beaten
  there were the Celts the Huns the Romans of old
and each has left something behind
  mostly a village burnt to the ground

Reared where I was and at forty
　　one peels roughly the apple called poetry
and is curious about the hidden kernel
　　beneath the ornaments the phrasing the intonation
and what is he to do if all the lesson of a bloody story is this
　　that Forgiveness Is With The Gods and Let's Love Each Other
　　　　Folks
Sure I'd say with all my heart
　　but what about the troublesome details
O liberty who are often yourself a prison guard
　　and perpetrate nasty acts and are not always the loyal lover
　　　　of beauty
but even when speaking in black skin and with the faulty grammar
　　　　of strong dialect
　　are the only possible hero of every poem worth the name
in the cage of the world where wrapped in the cloak of flesh shivers
　　　　the imagination
　　whose exploding nucleus is always the workaday
I have survived a siege what else could I believe in Under
　　the barbed wire of years a tin can and a jack-knife are poetry itself.

[WJS/LTA]

26

Snowfall in Boston

everything began here
and not just with the Tea Party
the rebels scalding the tea leaves (and before that the
taxes) of His Royal Majesty with icy harbour water
and not even on this continent
the city layout testifies to this clearly
with its English brick houses on the soil of Indian huts
and in the John Harvard Library of Cambridge Massachusetts
the name recalling king-beheader Cromwell

the moral is not to be found here of course
it's snowing in Boston
the cars skid on Boylston Street
and under Beacon Hill salty slush is tanning the boots
and the city is slurping the rushing flakes
of heavenly hopes as black mud soup
where the golden dome of the State House flickers

the moral is not an English tailor shop
nor is it the historic buildings
Indian Negro and all sorts of other blood has firmly hardened here
and in Chicago along Lake Shore Drive the highrises line up like
        launching pads
guard in the doorway cameras follow the visitor around
and there is always a plane above a certain point of Lake Michigan
and the penthouse bar slowly rotates and the waitress has no skirt on
and New York white collar workers carry with them a five kilo
        newspaper in the morning
of the five four is advertisement

so let's not soak in the centuries
let's go warm up in the Aquarium
the *superb infringement* will here not slip out of its *course*
what's more propelling his torpedo-shaped body with streamlined fins
he calmly circles behind the thick glass
and doesn't go hiding his voracious nature in books
as does history red with the blood of ideas

everything began here
and now everything is in vain
as usual it will end elsewhere and as something else
while above Boston there dumbly circles
with bone-cracking teeth in its gaping mouth
blasting aquariums
and untamable the large white shark
Winter

[TKS]

Requiem

He tossed a life preserver to the young castaway in '55
a longish first translation job for the bedhopping ingenu
about this monster poem says he
it's an epic shtik you can live off it meanwhile
he'd remembred me as the precocious monkey

the years then
our years on earth
first shooting then silence is all it is
up close everything seems small-time
but seen from a distance
as though one thumbed through Revelations
between a bloodypimpled sky and burning houses
we both aged
a pair of family men

I have my notion of Resurrection
the angel reeling off the official text
took me for someone else when
he pinned the brass medal
to my rib

the afterlife 1964
raining windy
K's coming from the direction of the Tuileries
his sweater blooming as big as the Czar's Bell
its hem hanging on him like a skirt
he says *let's sit down someplace before we freeze*

Sainted Trinity of paupers
he Julie and I
pooling our francs on payday
laughing as though we lived it up
and we are alive because we've invented immortality
(the kind we can afford)
a bottle of rosé

[JK/MK]

Certain Years

And down came the years one after another
    like black clouds We might as well start like this
It's a straight line from here to poetry so-called
    His The-Beautiful-is what-pleases-without-exciting-the-passions
        poem
sprinkled with a vision rising out of the kneadingtub
    and naturally a star's always welcome as a raisin
in the universal coffeecake for its light alone shining
    on the sentence Everything seems
okay Image after image 100% of capacity
    And the city where I grew fearfully wise
emerging after the war Lips shut
    eloquent eyes No meat Mother coming home with an empty
shoppingbag And in the pesticidal movie the newsreel's
    black-and-white dazzling with the future's Once-upon-a-time

It's easier this way Not raising the question
    are people to be blamed for what happens to them
And if they are because one way or another they are
    how and for how long? How big's the individual share of blame
the collective? And where do the stories start?
    What conqueror wan't conquered once?
And which of the conquered wouldn't prefer conquering?
    And who hasn't a good excuse for anything?
But if everything's merely a link in the chain reaching to the
        primordial cell
    what's this acrid flavour in my mouth? Whose blood?

I recall I'd just stepped off the sidewalk The burst
    nearly flung me against the wall I saw his face
Like mine the scared face of a child He just hangs onto
    the machinegun and mows away Any set of years
anywhere You squeeze yourself into the future between two years
    the barking harrying your heels You know him that
improviser capable of the lesser of two evils
    or an inexplicable good His own prisoner To that extent free
around the monkeyface blooming on the poster tacked to the Earth
    glory radiating everywhere.

[JK/MK]

30

On the Death of the Poet László Nagy

now the ragged wolf is still shaking the bloody hunk of flesh between
    its teeth
and our faces are holed by tears pattering like red-hot pebbles
and all our cells sing out like tomtits Latsi Latsi
let me make it plain that the poet
who pays with his life for every line he writes
couldn't care less about poetry otherwise
and would not say leaning his elbow on the tablecloth
that Federico this and Attila that
his poem if a poem is life itself
and nothing less than the endless tangle untied to the grave
even the greatest ideas relate to the simplest tool-kit
and it is well-known who repaired the bedposts back home
who turned this and that on a lathe and on one occasion
with the aid of a craftsman
smelted metal even
you were beautiful and not only to the eye
the soul itself rejoiced to see you living
because the years had carved your face not to a worthy headstone
    but into sculpture
because you were clever too yes clever
not in the same way as those too clever by half
but in a deeper and truer sense
possessing nature's formative momentum
which developed man from the protozoon
a poor one if you could only look back now
from the reverberating bosom of our atom-mother
to see your last invention
the secret of your posterity
around our black and swollen lips smashed in by a boxer
your indestructible smile

[AD]

31

To Poetry

Mesterségem, te gyönyörü
(My art, my delectation)
AGNES NEMES NAGY

My art, my delectation...?
My art, my arse!
This stubborn growth, this irritation,
This scratching place.

My salad days of faith
In art, in passion
Are past, or wear another face –
Art's my profession.

And poets survive, comme ci,
Comme ça – but me
I've little left to burn. You'll see
A spark of fury,

A world stiffened by spite,
Some frozen boughs
Observed down telescopic sights,
Through half-shut eyes.

But 'art, my delectation...'?
Of course, it's true.
Something beyond mere passion
Burns briefly through

The world of all-there-is,
Past form, past lust –
The shot deer pants and scurries,
Then hits the dust.

[GS]

A Fine Summer Day

I will carefully examine what I may see but once,
the sea of matter in a common streetscape.
And I will listen for the ubiquitous muttering of bedrock,
        the stunned battering of the whale's heart.
The here-and-now unlocks nowhere and never
through whose keyhole we may see earth's radiance of thinning hair,
a wrinkled nape of tarmac baked by the Parcae's silence.

[GS]

And their scattered bones will shine

And their scattered bones will shine –
felt not the stones in their shoes,
even if upon their feet, they had no shoes,
and no age, occupation, children:
threaded through each other's gaze, as in a needle,
they staggered like drunkards;
was feared they would fall flat,
as among the red-faced glowing fruit,
they themselves hung fruitlike,
drunk with glory and ridiculous...

And their scattered bones will shine –
the squeezed guttural sound, clouded pupils,
the personal details embodying the bodiless whole,
for them alone significant;
the infinite/and thus the finite/becomes,
from abstract notion, fuzzy touchable velvet:
a green jungle-blast in inter-stellar space,
and in the foaming leaf and liana-cascade
the Earth's hidden nature is visible,
a fireball lightning from dark panther cheeks...

And their scattered bones will shine –
now they are the universe, fish in water,
but also rippling water around fish;
adverbs of place lose meaning:
falling, rising, swirling,
in each other, from each other, through each other,
swishing on one spot neither-up-nor-down;
now thundering sweat rolling into valleys,
now the deaf sky above chattering teeth:
full emptiness, shiny faced raving darkness...

And their scattered bones will shine –
on the X-ray plate of an open fracture,
sparkling spinal column, generations;
their footfalls covered by the incessantly
shifting quartz-sand of the time-desert,
yet a raindrop-sized cell continues to recall:
there is eternity as long as there is death,
and in eternity they'll wander on a pebbly path,
and as if the wind blew from the village,
their hair will flutter, blissfully.

[GG]

The Caravan Rests for the Night

A desert shuddering in the bleak half-light.
The Creature born under the Sign of the Earth is sweating and
    snoring.
The demon cackles and shows clips from movies.

His first shows a lissom blonde aged seventeen who writhes
and braces her arms behind her moaning NO NO
but what she is thinking is *Get hold of my breast.*

On the second a disembodied mouth hovers above a man's lap
like a thirsty snake, its tongue downy with feathers,
which sucks from the velvet groin the spine that runs beneath it.

The third shows a naked post-coital couple who seem to have
    dropped from a height,
and through their hearts, as in some gothic novel, a wooden-handled
    kitchen knife,
their bodies, the bed, the room, the curtain, everything covered in
    blood.

The rest shows nothing, no one. Stygian darkness. Loud snoring.
The moon rises and pours metal into the deep creases of a face that
    was recently smooth.
The blanket of dust above the skeletons billows in the currents of cool
    air.

[GS]

Sinking Orpheus

(for Sándor Weöres on his 75th birthday)

The sober mind is annoyed to discover that poetry's utterly
    functionless.
Defending the defendable, it sings of the doormat and puts it by the
    door:
the dying poet lies on his side on the ground
and writes in the dust with his blood the word: *heimat!*
But should this scenario fail,
for lack, let us say, of a Struggle for Independence,
he is still permitted to sing of the scheduled reforms -
the government's or the opposition's - whichever appeals to him.
The sober mind, as we know,
(to use its own favourite expression)
with its indispensible aids to survival,
the various clichés for use in case of fire, flood or earthquake,
resides in the collective unconscious, or numbskull.

I rarely took tea at the genius's table.
Nature had wrought a Mozartian miracle in his wren-like body
– perhaps on a whim, perhaps on purpose to demonstrate
that not every question has an answer. Our conversation
had the quickfire wit of a comedy of manners: *More tea for you
my dear Ottó? – Oh no, thank you, no.*
The flame is on Low, but it burns all the same. Dwarf candlestick,
    the everyday creature
was with me one minute, nowhere the next, wavered and rose and
    then fell
through the mysterious medium in which
a gabbling angel dictates down the phone, and the poem is ready for
    printing
and from the thick bog a slippery presentiment floats to the surface
serrated teeth, reptilian neck, and shark's fin,
most monstrous of monsters, the soul.

Orpheus the diver. He scrapes the skin of the age and it scrapes him,
but human suffering is merely the air in his cylinder,
the essence of his mastery is this: that the depths are a freight
    on his poems:
down in the depths is a shadow, a ship that went down,

around it no coins, no amphorae, only the darkness within things,
and within that still denser, the darkness of genesis,
infinity contained in a mere point of fire –
though infinity's not made of points: everything wavers,
only the wind, only the whirling, only the flux remains firm...
Seekers of treasure, we circle a sunken star with its torso of light,
while empires stream by in a pearled string of bubbles,
and above us the ocean of time is pulsing with light.

[GS]

On the Death of István Vas

Last night, István Vas, being dead
fate wound up his file on the poet,
found his name in his vast A–Zed,
and wrote cancelled clearly below it.
The data were not much to go on,
not such as to do a man honour:
eyes: staring, jaws: wide and so on,
in other words, *this one's a goner.*

Can anything comfort or ease us?
Where's God, in our great desolation?
He vanishes as if to tease us,
like the man in K's Funeral Oration.
But one thing is certain: we laughed
and sat in his garden together,
leant back in our chairs, and I quaffed
his whisky and talked of the weather.

And I saw he was brave although scared,
a hero despite of his terror,
like one whom disgust had prepared
at the century's terrible mirror,
as a Jew a primitive Christian,
as a Christian a pagan-discursive;
there lurked in his soul beyond question
a gentle and courteous subversive

one true in his heart, and effectual:
respected for wit and incision,
a naiviste intellectual,
a poetic metaphysician
who bedded the proud and the pretty,
till body was pleasured and glutted,
who courted his capital city
like a lover with beauty besotted,

the city, that bounteous sewer
of festering spirit and matter,
you, murderous country, you were
his love and his only begetter:
never mind that the road in its motion
leads nobody no place whatever,
that deluge and revolution
relieve us not here and not ever.

Stumbling through night, he rehearses
laments that he wrote for another,
who lived, as does he, in his verses,
our Pista, our father and brother:
no pills in his pockets, but merely
the torch of his poems to ease him,
to lighten his circuit so clearly
mortality may predecease him.

[GS]

2. The Blood of the Walsungs

Wild Beast

A wild beast roars from the walls of buildings. Arrrgh, cries the terrible voice. Arrrgh, answers the whole city with the secret and uncontrollable horror of circus lions. Eeek, the frightening neon signs shriek, frightened. Arrrgh, howl admirals, professors, musical directors and foremen. Arrrgh, howls the husband with a horrible fear in his heart at his sluttish wife. Arrrgh, the latest model cars and towering trucks howl at old ladies and blind old men. Arrrgh, scream the frightened military courts, contagious diseases, tombstones, professional bounders and memorials to the Unknown Soldier. Arrrgh, arrrgh, comes the drawn-out roar with a slight pause for a breather of the entire mountain and valley all tamed by power lines. Meanwhile the sun, humming and tickling, sits on people's noses, buildings, signs. Arrrgh, the city, frightened to the point of tears, roars at the sun. What can you do, the sun has been sitting there four or five years now and for who knows how much longer. It's noon.

[JB]

Painting

I have always been depressed. I carry Nero's eyes six feet off the ground, above a flame-red beard and a crooked nose. What a pair of eyes, I should know. A ballerina looked into their depths and danced in front of me for five miles on a highway between two villages in the lakeshore night, just to cheer me up. But I remained depressed and asked her to marry me. On the rare occasions I still think of her I know it is better this way, alone. They say my hair is red although no one has ever seen it; I go around wearing a hat under the radiant sky, I even sleep in it. Only at night, when the holiday-makers get lost and turn off their radios and the midgets appear on the shore, do I grow: I stare out over the gigantic trees. I draw a self-portrait with a single unending line between sky and earth. A strange picture, but not at all scary, melancholy rather. You stop under it and muse, how infinite sadness is! But this too is fleeting. Dawn always arrives faster than you think, hills of cheap bed-linen rise from underground. – Good morning, Mr Anthony! the landlady cheerily greets me.

[JB]

Rowing Boat

The rowing boat – let's not see each other again! – slipped its moorings. Now in this all-spray, all-foam, all-mirror-tower, all-glass-valley, all-flood world, tied to the weak song of an orphan seashore …This is how love sinks in the propeller-tasting water. I sailed for three years running from the great flood. I left behind a child, a one-story house. O, O the merciless sea! they are tolling Swinburne's cardboard bells in a long-sunk cathedral. And who receives a finer funeral music? You can mourn an old neighbourhood, the memorable breasts of a past love, the blade of grass in your mouth, a real tough brawl. Hardly anything else. Here an eternal peace hums, a godless dynamo or heavenly waterfall, it is none of your business; you see only the deserted cities celebrating in the blinding light, the barren factory yards, melting into a single oceanic smile or the grimace of lamentable rocks. But does it matter? You would have never believed that the radiance could become so uncontrollable, that all slag is burnt out of your bones, all pity, hunger and homecoming.

[JB]

Sea Grass

I imagine the scent of sea grass.

It will be a song, like any bird's but more graceful and prodigious. Like an arrow, a wingless swoosh.

But the world at hand puts a spell on me: O, O the god of dawn awakening hums from behind golden stubble. His living saints fly out of soapsuds, and in the ragged temples of his tea-scented smile tiny statues of black Magi with closed eyes start on their pilgrimage toward the morning star of Bethlehem.

And... I almost forgot! they are installing a crane on the street and the goddam foreman is being cussed out because a wing screw is missing and what is a crane without a wing screw. Something too horrible to think of!

So many miracles deserve another. The smell of sea grass flooding through the window.

[JB]

A Photo

Somebody takes me by the hand. She's a large-eyed, black woman, perhaps my mother. The sunshine falls in torrents on the jetty and somebody takes me by the hand, me in my girl's dress that I've outgrown. It's Mother. Who am I? We roamed the spruce forest like wild animals, wolfed down the leaves of green shrubs. We, daughters of nature, primeval ecstasy, we kicked, we bit when they found us. An immigrant family took us in. I forgot my mother tongue. There were wars here and we were always fleeing. I call a stranger *Mother*. Not even one drop of water on earth calls me *Orphan*. Nowhere do I see a jetty or sunlight! the wind roves above my head toward new ports. I passed through villages that belonged to the savage: I clawed like a cat. I came to ruin in a quiet city, my belly grew from the shriek of pleasure. Haycarts, trains, cheap bedroom furniture. I'm in a small country on the perimeter of Europe. I drink strong coffee. I'm thinking of my child: it would be good to pull in with her to this port. Mother would wave to us from the shore in her summer dress that's been out of fashion for years. 'You came home?' she'd ask. 'Yes,' I'd say. We would drink milk in her house and eat bread. I can hate so deeply that my mouth and hair throw off sparks. There will be no forgiveness!

[NK]

The General

The morning of the General. It's a miserable morning. Starts with constipation. Then comes the nail clipping, the shampoo. Then you rush immediately to catch the parade. Of course, the headstand don't wash this time. One year before retirement: perpetual fear and trembling. 'Soldiers,' he bursts into tears, 'there is too much VD around here.' Then the foot inspection. Then the sharp-shooting exercise, with cannon on human targets. Ten, twenty dead, but always some shop windows get broken here and there, and that's what they always make a big deal out of. The requisitioning of glass, the documents, the insurance – it wears down your nervous system. Then the flame-throwers malfunction, the corpse-transportation isn't working, you can't park because of the traffic. You have to drag the corpses by string on the sidewalk – expensive and time-consuming. What can you do, it's peacetime. Then you have to take the medicine in order to make your stools rock-hard and right-angled. Then there's no time for anything, running home lunchtime. 'AttenSHUN!' shouts a one-year-old at the doorway. That's right, there's plenty to pay attention to. You call this a life?

[LB/MN]

An Excursion

Came to the hills with Martha. The city no longer suited her hair: it had turned black in the everlasting sunlight, like a kind of sad gaiety. I thought, – Here's the place to bring her. We started off in the morning in a crowd of baskets, chickens, people. I said to her, – It's like this, you see. And she was silent, in one corner of her mouth a faint smile, like a plant. I imagined her breasts in her blouse. We walked like that for three hours. On top of the hill she got scared. – A bug! she shrieked with an accusatory terror, wrapping her skirt tightly round her. She was a city girl, she couldn't imagine what that big family was like. We lay down in the grass anyway. A game of lust, the unrestrained glare dealing out such sweet cards that we lost it all, slaves of chance. But could I ever have thought of that? She stared at me with utterly empty eyes: I felt not a touch of remorse. A train carried her off. Then years of silence at the station. Nothing in particular changed: the engines whistled, creaked – soundlessly. Silence flowed from the gaping mouth of the newsdealer. In an armchair I fell for twenty years, accelerating downwards. But touched ground: I exist. No big deal after all.

[JK/MK]

A Blade of Grass

I'm a blade of grass between your lips! It too is the Son of God, it too is crucified by Spring, and rises again in Winter's fury: how fiery just one breath is! I was happy here, you know. We walked all one summer in the hidden paths of elder and wild strawberries: love cooled in me like a mole, and sunlight too sank underground so that I had to sip you up from between slick clods. And that too, where is it now? The wind off the sea grieves for our unforgettable tans; we can't go there again: we're happy somewhere else. The river is visible from the hilltop; not one word can you utter from our final home: instead of youth's well-water, we drink the smoke of barges forever. But – you're beautiful, you're beautiful – I shout in the flawed wreckage, in the ruined autumn woods. I hold you in my mouth as water does the sunken ship. And it's good; why should I wish to be somewhere else? I glimpsed a happy city; the sea cast it up; the shore buried it; and it knew no more than this one blade of grass between my teeth. Our life dies away among green pleasures.

[JK/MK]

A Memorable Fancy

'Shipwreck in the washtub. The commonest of all stories. The story of a woman. Of my sagging breasts and flabby belly. Of fatigue in my veined thighs. Permanent waves sail greasily around my head in the steam of lean meals. In the trade winds of kitchen drafts and Gulf Streams of laundry. Columbus of dirty underwear, I stare out of the window and – land! land! – out of the unbelievable sea of forty years the cobblestone courtyard rises to the surface. Actors, scenes in a dumb play. 'I'm going crazy' – a boy tumbled me in the grass. The joy of my bones sparkled in his teeth. Raving locomotives over our heads. One spark set my skirt on flame. Years, whirlpools, rivers. Days, days on the sea of mistakes. Doodads, furniture on the waves of old age. 'Sweetheart you look marvellous!' Tomorrow I will rise early. I will lie down on a lacy tombstone.'

[JB]

Note

'I saw her today. She stepped in front of me from behind a kiosk, wearing an old-fashioned winter coat. Some vague recognition commiserated on my face. An inhuman shame. The street, like a fit of fever, took possession and began to murder: an awkward wingbeat, a child's. If only I could have escaped! I would remember other cities, as if I had been there: the river armoured by the sun like a crusader. In the water, green branches and drowning fruit. And not this snowy railway terminal – I've had an operation, she said, they found a tumour in my stomach, I am over the worst. The fever herded me toward the port. Through the slushy passageways of a can of sardines reaching to the sky. In her mouth, where the saliva of delight had swirled once and the boat of my lewd tongue had crashed on the teeth – a black gap. Drought, drought in the heart. – I am really glad to hear that, I replied.'

[JB]

To Be Poor

To be poor, even just relatively poor, means that a man lacks the brashness to decorate his speech with Christmas-tree baubles and hold forth to the fighters of a war on the whistling wings of gorse. To be poor is to have an irresistible wish to answer yes or no if we are questioned. To be poor is to wade barefoot through the splintered-glass sea of technology and hand-feed a lion equipped with every modern convenience. To learn an upside-down ethics, to discover everything about the concealed dungeons of a sky-bound earthscraper; to crawl backwards along the narrowing corridors of the cavern of history into that primordial workshop where blood and wretchedness are pounded into Ariel-shapes of humaneness. To be poor in a world where Romeo is a car and Juliet a cosmetic may be an embarrassing merit but it is also a happy embarrassment, for the poor man lives in the besieged stronghold of thought without relying on any possible safe-conduct, and instead he gallops bareback on an earth with its mane flying and he uses his patient anger to spur it on its way.

[EGM]

Concert

As they surround the house, there is no mistaking their expertise.
No superfluous gesture. No false step. All goes with classic simp-
licity as in some baroque piece of music or in a dentist's chair. An
operation, not a manhunt. Rifles at the ready, at ease, steps right
and left, as at a dancing school. This way, please, after you – a
thrust barely noticeable yet firm between the shoulderblades, no
touch of refined cruelty. A minuet of machines: traffic moving to
perfection. Diesel-rondos, khaki-sonatas. After formless agony an
elegy of relief: the wind rinsing the houses. Blood-clotted tufts of
weeds, sputum of mud-walls dotting a cuplike village. Standing out
like a Greek idea on the autumn anarchy the colonnade of goose
steps. A marching masterpiece. In the Alpine purity of measure
and proportion is celebrated the practice of generations. O brushes!
O chisels! O arrested movements! No ordinary moment: the hunter
and the hunted on the same plinth of a hill. The dénouement is
more prosaic. The house as if on second thought thrusts high its
roof, then falls flat on the ground steaming like a cow-flop. Dust
circles for a while before clearing away. One error on the map,
and earth the wiser for it.

[WJS/LTA]

From Very Close

I had been a battery commander and lived and slept with the dull crack of guns. A hand, a foot flew by at times. During the collapse of the army in 1919, we took up our position in a small town. 'Men, there will be order from now on!' I said. Later I was arrested, got a fancy trial. One of the spectators said: 'A lawyer's son, a reactionary.' The war, a revolution, years of peace, exile – these are the weekdays of our era of earthquakes. Once they shackled my hands to my feet and suddenly my back started to itch. I recall exactly that it itched below my shoulder blade. At first I barely felt it, but later it became quite agonising. Finally, it itched so hard, I almost went mad. Then I got married; I took a thin, big-boned woman for my wife. We lived in a village and had chickens. I think we loved each other. Then disease took the life of my son. My wife died of sorrow. My hand began to shake then; I became homesick. When my sister first saw me, she could only say: 'Oh, my God!' 'Well,' I told her, '35 years is a long time.' Then we just stared at each other, two old wrecks, ailing with rheumatism. Sometimes, I muse about having witnessed a turning point in our times. I recall, for example, how beastly my itch was. I can't even describe it. I could only think: SCRATCH! I don't throw away dry bread. My whole apartment – under the bed, the kitchen shelves, the table – is filled with dry bread that I've wrapped in paper.

[NK]

A Love Match

Ours was a love match. We sat on a mountain ridge and peered down at the Danube. May, the prodigal, bathed earth in its green barrel. The river ground with its waves the Turkish sword of Szentendre Island. 'You see,' I told her. 'I'm incurably attached to this piece of earth.' We hardly said more. I clasped her breast as delicately as if it were a living ciborium. Later she gave birth to my children. But we weren't overcome by drudgery or ennui. We didn't tire for years of the rapture we offered each other. What burst inside us and in which of us? The worst thing was that our double bed still deluded us after three years of mutual carnage. I sensed that she was clinging to me now with more ardour than once on the mountain ridge – is she cheating on me with myself? Lust tormented me. It felt awfully good! I hated us both. Then even this passed. Now a tired woman sets the table for supper. I gaze at the chalice of my madness like a gloating insect collector: she has the same face, the same body! Prodigal May. Turkish sword? We're the clowns of our own fate and the unhealable nostalgia can be cured on the spot. One can only be a poet on paper.

[NK]

The Blood of the Walsungs

Retired Uncle Miksa glittered like a sword in the sheath called life.
He used to be a showcase Jew at Novara and he was proud of it.
His nod was a salute as he spoke about his brother-in-arms, His
Grace the Prince. During the monarchy, he married his first cousin
after the Emperor had given his consent. He sired two daughters.
Exemplary order reigned in his house: breakfast was served at 7:30
and lunch promptly at noon. The daughters had the same mouths
and eyes as other girls. Only their husbands they chose from
among the mad. One committed suicide at the beginning of 1947.
He was a manic-depressive and a dashing hotel owner. They later
nationalised his elegant hotel. The other husband, when he had an
attack and foamed at his mouth, crawled to the window to jump
out. But reaching the edge of the windowsill, he fainted. This man
was brimming with life when he was normal. The paprika sauce
of the pork stew glinted on his chin. Uncle Miksa didn't live to
see this; he died before the Nurnberg Rulings on Rehabilitation
took their effect. He didn't experience the co-habitation of families
– the partition curtain in the hallway of the apartment. He didn't
meet the ex-filmmaker, our sedate boarder, who slept on a rug
where his hands were stepped on. He didn't read the accusations to
the authorities, didn't appear as a witness in the trial of his daughter.
The waves of filth around the dining room table escaped him. Also
the scuffle of the lost for the rickety furniture. As is becoming a
mariner, his photo persisted, fastened to the wall. In these times of
misfortune. Uncle Miksa embodied metaphysics – the new Odin
of Szondi street.

[NK]

Chile

The patrol came down without having found anything. 'The third time they've been,' said the woman, 'and found nothing.' 'Cheerio, kid,' the lieutenant said to the child. 'We won't be here again.'

'Why, did you find daddy in the attic?', the child asked. 'We did,' said the lieutenant and went back into the house and brought the man down and shot him dead in the yard in front of the child and the woman.

Pupils stare like great worlds: the Earth, in its green dress, tells lies about sea and spring, surrounded by the searing stars.

[EGM]

Europe

I have always backed off from the word.
In the Thirties Europe meant French. But was it only then?
Not in earlier centuries? A bloody lesson learned that Europe was
Balmazujváros as well as Notre Dame!
But in America I was European. And not because of megalopolis
the size of regions, and so on. The difference was never size. My
time reared us as an easy going builder with millenial movements.
Peoples on peoples, ideas on ideas, a house was erected and a stable
and secret tracks adjusted by later blueprints. Beginning and end
met as ever on that Continent. And at the end of those secret
passages, some ray of light... some fixed idea...for what else is
hope? But what am I doing here elsewhere with T's grandfather
who yelled at the Nazi slamming the boxcar door on him We are
living in a constitutional state! Protein chain of contradictions
stretched between two worlds, live wire between burst of laughter
and mourning, I went to the window with nothing better to do,
looked at the Iowa River roll the Indian name in its poison-green
waters slowly southwards.

[EM]

58

A Small Country: 1

I too was duped about poetry being omnipotent...We have no ocean? Let's invent one. The Danube glinted green. Viki listened ecstatically to my latest adolescent poem. I expected the melon rind to float past me as it did for Attila József. But time only vomited flames and the metallic clicking so characteristic of an earlier age. Years later we met again at the Lukács pool in Budapest. One couldn't detect on her the prison years. She's all right, she said. Got married. They erased her criminal record, at least promised that. We have one life and one death. This means in a small country: *one* pool, *one* authority and *one* projection room where the film profession congregates. And the film on the screen is a study of a family tree where everybody is related to everybody and the concepts ABOVE and BELOW are provisional because an unforeseeable change could come and make everything stand on its head and reveal the fact that there has been no change. In the treadmill meanwhile ample blood splashes – well, we're gathering grapes...A few photos with black borders: souvenirs, epitaphs. We quickly forget them and sunbathe on the rim of a volcano. HOWDY, HOW THE HECK ARE YOU?...THANKS, I'M FINE...Should I have said that there's still time to remedy things?...I stopped reading poems to women. I don't believe that poetry is a care package dropped from a helicopter among those in a bad way. The poem, like a bloodhound, is driven by its instincts after the wounded prey. But the latter will change form and essence on the run: go ahead, catch the real anguish in the act! You follow the trail of probability's interstellar Mafia, the trail of the Black Hand, who had spun a gas cloud (torn from the sun) as if it were a lottery wheel – this way inside the cloud, a massacre and a tourist path could intersect. It cajoles, with a reasonable image of the future, a passion for gambling.

[NK]

A Small Country: 2

A Central European hell. None of Dante's Latin exaggeration; even though some sort of juice bubbles in the basin between the great mountain ranges, it's a geyser, not a tar pool. Instead of demons turning spits, merely a troop of globetrotting tourists gushes from the bus. Yes, some scraping of brakes and teeth. Otherwise the arrangement's first-class. And the view's perfect for a picture post-card, no fooling; cliffs here, undulations there, a plain beyond, and on them always the particular century's props: castle, clay-and-wattle church, TV tower. And peoples lying atop each other like rocks. Deep drilling's a favourite amusement, to demonstrate which stratum was laid down earliest. Aside from that, the main business is keeping accurate accounts, newborns to be later transferred from the *Income* column to other columns, depending on what turns out to be necessary just then: heroes, victims, et cetera. Note: it's easier for the bookkeepers if each generation's placed, when it comes to the bottom line, under *Loss*. Furthermore, note that the small country's panther doesn't give birth to a mouse; she delivers a panther, which for economy's sake is as small as a mouse. Still, there's no economising on one thing, and, as all visitors agree, the bloodied clouds offer marvellous vistas at sunset. Especially when, staring into the objective of the coin-binoculars, we observe that Caraffa, a Generalissimo of Italian lineage and Grand Marshal of the Imperial Army garrisoned on the high ground, writes a letter on a flying desk made out of a puff of haze ruffled in the Baroque manner, to Baron Jacob Julius Haynau: 'Greetings, dear cuz! I hear you've had them hanged. Wonderful! I myself prefer using tongs...'

[JK]

A Nice Little War

Of course a war would quickly solve our problems; Behemoth would answer: no more bald heads, no more surplus value, no new left, no question of sex, no community projects...The fever of youth could take a cold bath. Or one of fire. Why not? Imagine! the sea of swollen flame would stop before the cellar stairs. Imagine! those who have nothing would not be ruined by their losses... it would be their turn at last...the southern hemisphere would remain...Brasilia...this way madness lies. And not just because of the flattened steelworks or the mountains of corpses. We sought god and found ourselves; our limits; I am as I am because ultimately I cannot be anyone else. A clean sheet then? Inscribed with blood? If one could lean over the balcony of the stars this perhaps would prove our masterpiece: the pattern that dictates the passing of time. However, excessive objectivity disgusts me. It is precisely the smell of the earth that is divine in me; those I saw ploughing with wooden shares and tractors; the taut ocean begins to hum, and round it the reference points of the face of infinity...trees, pot-holes along the road, a centipede...as far as the world is concerned poetry is a matter of detail. I learned this during the storming of a city, the lesson took less than half an hour. At first we heard only the breathing. The wheezing of an enormous pair of lungs some distance off. Then we understood it was our lack of air pumping the live bellows in our chests. A vast silence followed. The sense of dizziness at having survived. An iron door. A gallery above. Mortar between clumsy stones. Later the silent film: coats covered in brick dust swaying at the resurrection ball... eyes drinking light like lidless mirrors...Could I look into another mirror now? The conquest of the world left me behind to act as messenger. The news burned up my lips as they were muttering: NO.

[GS]

The Spirit of the Age

I saw a beggar. Recognised him. Knew him instinctively. 'You have a damned nerve,' I cried and shook his shoulders in cold fury. 'You dare to poke your nose in here! Aren't you the liar who told us this would be positively the last struggle? Wasn't it you who promised every poet a redhead or red way ahead – to each according to his need?' I stood there for a long time screaming furiously... eventually he raised his hooded head and I saw he had no eyes. His hollow sockets were a keyhole opening on to a smooth and endless plain where fire and smoke mingled, and invisible feet pounded over a few exposed bones. It might have been cavalry or fugitives. There was the dreadful constant sound of something grinding. I couldn't tell whether it was a loose axle or a human cry, or if it was the earth scratching its bloody surface in the eternal drought that follows tears of suffering. Then he addressed me in a flat exhausted voice as if talking down a microphone. 'You think yourself a seer because you've been disappointed. And in your infinite wisdom you bawl at me like some cheap whore. You come back with your dowry, your naive ideas, your bloody revolution! Bring back God, the family, tradition, and kick me out! But are we not one person? And isn't your imagination the whole problem? The wheel of time remains indifferent, you are the squirrel in the cage rushing round on the wheel which like a lathe turns out the centuries.' He fell quiet and the wind dispersed him and nothing remained of him except the cooling ground where he had sat, and fire and smoke and dust.

[GS]

62

3. A Visit to Room 104

The Fire Breathing Bull

I was born under the sign of the bull: ponderous and explosive,
everything about me is bound to the body;
now that the body is cooling my confidence dwindles.
The bull imagines Bull as God: an inflamed eyeball,
his nostrils a saxophone blowing like wildfire –
the cell to whom life is a matter of studious craftsmanship
freely expanding its superfluous energy,
till nothing is left but the suction effect of a dented container,
the reverse side, a whirlpool of abstractions;
what can he do there, in that etherial medium
where ideas flaunt their parthenogenesis, sexless…
the dying volcano shudders at the memory of old eruptions
with their bubbling streams of molten lava:
above him the old miasma, image of the soul, smoke rolled by wind.

[GS]

A Middle Aged Man

Middle aged? The Middle Ages pictured a feudal hell
under an earth pricked out with Gothic imitations of heaven,
a world composed in a stiff hierarchy, where
the devil extracted his tithe with a pitchfork.
The sign of our times is the buzzing of a box:
technology tacking like a suicidal butterfly
in the limitless air of television screens...
We ourselves are always our own hell,
the scrubbed prophet of heaven locates it in the future...
Reality is the surface of the planet, landscapes
that dissolve into each other, doubt, hope: a tiny globe
in a child's hand, who'd rather use it as a marble...
To live is to blunder into a hole lined with burning embers
to believe the damp cell in the ovum stuttering: the future is yours.

[GS]

To Catullus

It's quite a gas, but we love Lesbia too, Catullus...
Youth, according to the rights of youth, imagines
its possibilities to be endless, to be itself a god.
Now God exists and now he doesn't, whatever youth desires;
when he drops off the earth spins on without its master.
Youth's only limit is health. The fact is that
we're slow on the uptake: we would always rather
catch the cosmic fish in the ocean of the stars,
while all the time the blue-whale flashes us a sharp kiss
from our cells. Our bodies cheat us, alas, the bestial whores,
they lie that everything will remain as it is, only transformed
behind a moving veil of light as in a speeding comet's wake:
the living fire, the madness, thighs beaten to cream...
Can we do better than believe in them?

[GS]

Individualism

In my youth I wanted to be an original,
and so I stole from Ginsberg and Pilinszky;
I waited for them to turn the corner, then zap...
Today I sniff at the teeming fishpond of anthologies;
images, images, and what is it all worth?
It was not greed that led me on to Lowell;
five years I spent translating the so-called sonnets,
and it never occured to me to write the like –
it was only when I could not finish typing up a page
and in my need searched for similar distances in other minds,
like a painter who takes the brush in his mouth...
I am a poet, such as I am, not a particularly cheering sight;
on everything I do I leave my mark: my dying right-hand's
little catscratch waiting for its cryptogramatist.

[GS]

Josephus

Ever more wrinkles on the beloved face,
ever less vitality in the passion –
the grey Fury rushes up and down in her flaming nightie
Where is my youth, so dearly purchased?
I note down everything, like Josephus in wartime:
'This morning an inflammation of the spine,
vertebrae minced by bladed siege-machinery,
body like kindling with a headache
drawn inch by inch into the icy embers of numbness.'
If there were a God that I could grasp
he would exist between two worlds, in an age of changing values,
and be like me, a stubborn, man-made creature:
his world is bodged, each nut and bolt misplaced,
but clings to hope, the coming generations.

[GS]

from One-Time Loves

My one-time loves, if I could meet you now,
as you then were, what would I fall in love with?
I'd prick your thousand faults out at one go,
your prinking and your pseudish cleverness, your whoring.
How can I get my body to function, to play the volcano
which used to cover your Pompeian thighs, like lava?
For which of you now would I smash up the call-box,
if she's at home (and she wasn't) *why won't she answer?*
Youth is not merely a military campaign conducted by atlantes
but a lazer beam of obsessions;
Romeo wears his blinkers like a dray-horse –
true that he later tries to tear them off,
to see the frozen fields of bone beneath the moonlit arcades.
Everything is relative, the saw screams to the branch.

[GS]

Around My Stony Cradle

Illyés did not like Budapest –
of course he lived in Budapest at the time,
and not where he said the worthwhile people lived.
For my part, cruising these streets some fifty years
is like living with a woman you don't know,
precisely because you know her all too well...
Love has always been adept at contradictions;
I've seen so many towns, I'm dripping with them,
but only one I've seen in ruins: her,
her uncombed hair of grey smoke straggling over her brow,
and under her torn furs the tanks creeping like lice...
I'll never forget while I live, how she shook herself, spring of 45,
the small-time whore in her skirt of light. Hope lures
the future to her foul mattress and winks: *You coming, kid?*

[GS]

Resurrection

For three long years the tom-cat played with me,
and taught me what his daughters taught King Lear.
Now drugs drive me towards my resurrection
on routes preferred by mice – with parked cars either side
treading each other down. It's Hungary and 1984.
Just one more minute, one more day, one year...
It's what every founder of religion says.
When I twigged that life was more important than verse
I thought that I could manufacture gold,
poems that were not verse, but life entire;
a thousand times we've played the fool, believed it
and tried to shift the ocean with holed buckets.
I live. The sun above me has a tiger face,
its beams are whiskers trembling. They scent blood.

[GS]

In the Cathedral at Uppsala

Who in God's name would think to call up here
I queried in the nave on hearing the wild
insistent telephone ringing in the sacristy;
the po-face creased, the rest burst out in laughter...
Honest to God, I got drunk on being alive,
on feeling my mind turning, my hand moving...
But he who in my frivolity I had imagined at the dial,
that smoky, bitter, dark, unbending lutheran
with the chill of predestination in his bones,
even if outraged, simply put down the receiver:
he'd seen this often enough, the grasshopper's green lightning
sucked into the flames of a bush burning like alcohol –
and then the same, now sober, crippled and hobbling in the wind,
till all things fade: youth, fame, *zeitgeist*, summer.

[GS]

Off Season at a Swedish Resort

Could a mature man desire a more fitting place of rest
than this landscape with its coat of snow?
Iron posts mark out the road in both directions,
the boats arranged on ramps, Venice on a sleigh –
that Mediterranean *douce et léger*, but framed in ice...
Earth, sea, summer, sleep with cotton buds stuffed in their ears...
I too am sleeping in an armchair in an electrically heated house:
the few years that are left, I'll sleep away,
like the world, which the Baltic wind peoples with mad knives...
O mamma mia, the Italian waiter hiding in my body
mumbles in his sleep, *what about the good old stink of home?*
Can one live without the image of lost causes?
In a rational world, without patrons and assassins?
Can one enjoy spaghetti with bottled ketchup?
A future half-baked without the spice of madness?

[GS]

Night Call

This will be just like that crazy telephone call
before midnight in the tropics, in the hotel in Delhi;
I wake from a black sea that rocks the purring lifeboat
of the air-conditioning, I'm silver as a flying fish,
I speak neither English nor Hungarian,
only my splitting gills help me to bear the shower
of words, that begging, aggressive, otherworldly voice:
come here at once, I want to sleep with you!
This will be the same, except I won't put down the receiver
or turn to the wall, but shall put on my shirt and trousers;
I know who it is, that oriental look cannot disguise her;
I've waited for you, the door opens, its hinges are centuries,
and her black hair glows with a blue flame and covers everything;
a thin line of smoke escapes through the keyhole, that was me...

[GS]

Verdi in Old Age

Art has always been a treacherous terrain;
the audience, a thousand-headed caesar
with a glowing pumpkin mask across each face
tends to prefer a bathtubful of spilt blood
to that single drop trembling on the grasses of a score:
Jawohl, Wagner's revolutionary band of firemen thunders on...
Should the child born in the war become a tight-lipped ancient?
Then so be it. The ember on my tongue is much like his,
that old demodé gentleman, guitarist, songbird;
the ridiculous part-paralysed Falstaff I've become
slaps a poem down on the bar table: *I'll fart you the Dies Irae,*
everyday life is the hidden key to everything;
I must still be young, since I once knew a wrinkled old dame
with green fire in her pores, a certain Giuseppina Strepponi.

[GS]

Before the Autumn Cull

Why should a bull suffer all these fancy diseases,
when his peasant mind can not cope with abstractions?
Both heaven and hell for him are merely fields,
one grows fine grass, the other burning thistles...
It makes me laugh when I consider my beliefs,
the great humane ideals, sheer nineteenth century,
and for all my reservations and parentheses
they are essentially blind, incurable.
I'm of that parting generation whose baptism of fire
bequeathed them epilepsy and a sense of solid values;
The moderns in their screaming nosedive showered us
with cream-puffs that exploded. I tasted them
and have been this way since, standing by the cellar,
light, light, infinite light and a fluttering, the wrecked yard.

[GS]

An Evening In

Tonight I'm ill again.
Mr Bones the undertaker swirls into the room –
the door is closed, the wall simply ignores him –
he stalks up and down, sits in my chair, tries on my glasses,
makes an objective assessment of my material circumstances:
'The result of years of work... a nice mess, all of it...
books piled to the ceiling, manuscripts strewn on the floor...'
I take no notice of him, but with tightly shut eyes
I summon images of life, the five great oceans,
a woman's face, as it flaps like a crazed bird
in blind ecstasy in a brilliant vacuum.
My icy breath steams up at the hot image;
Mr Bones wipes his brow, like me he can't bear the change in the
        weather:
'I'm going now. I was simply passing by. But I'll be back.'

[GS]

Local Customs

To write in a country where the tailor's yardstick
is sometimes thirty inches, sometimes forty,
is only just possible, granted good eyesight and a sound character.
Odysseus as a character? Not impossible perhaps –
providing we imagine Homer as a Greek who is part Byzantine.
The atmosphere is stifling, all that gold;
principle and anti-principle both aim at domination,
blindly, vengefully, like jealous women...
Is there any behaviour more provocative than being natural?
a sin more grievous, bargaining for what may yet be saved,
if all that could not turns out to shine with rarer brilliance?
The plump and bearded reader in philosophy, ponders beady eyed
above fields of wheat which have known both flood and drought,
There is no perfect weedkiller. Let's burn the lot.

[GS]

House and Home

A house, a home, Horatius, Illyés, indeed, *the lot...*
But chiefly the subterranean pool, freckled with silk and velvet:
an adolescent's image of earth's lap
or what lies beneath that triangle of grass –
the brimstone path to hell, that opalescent lake
with German tourists and chippies along its shore,
in which I dip myself each year to gauge
how much my life has managed to squeeze from me.
Summer: the rustic club is now a stalwart piston, the male member
proudly pumps the yielding medium, no problem;
he is happy to be his own way, truth and life –
great mushroom clouds cannot daunt the random explorer
whose mighty lightning zaps into the lap of the material;
followed by darkness and nothing, and nothing and darkness...

[GS]

Beneath the Thundering Roof
Hamline University, St Paul, Minnesota

No fantasy more inscrutable than that which exists;
what we claim to know is merely a membrane, oceans of cells either side –
too bad we should live our lives in terror of it
and so we pretend it is human, and give it a sense of humour...
Who knows what life should compensate us for, why now?
why war, why the hospitals, the diploma we failed to obtain?
Too late, too late, sniggers Professor Orbán of Hungary,
he has already felt the dark current of air, and even though crippled,
he is, compared to his mad teenage self, practically free...
Should he sell this for bits of luminous trash sold on television?
Here I sit in the golden age of the empire, the air-conditioning
      humming,
teaching the fraught psychology of vandals to simple-faced Romans –
more serious though is the roof, cracked and thundering with
      imperial aircraft,
which even the limestone column of my spine cannot shore up.

[GS]

That Dizzying Difference in Size

A big country: I can feel its vast body working,
the lung that expands from Canada to Mexico,
as it tightens expelling a myriad vehicles
into the afternoon chaos of peak-time traffic;
I change lanes, accelerate and brake –
one of the natives: part of the rhythm of mutual dependence...
one of the natives? Ridiculous! A case of the camel through the eye
        of the needle...
I like a lot of things here but nothing so much
as the fact that there's nothing more left here to envy –
which wonder of the world, if any, could change me
or deny that I am the principal thing the place is still missing:
such common-physical-contact, such tight-collar measures?
I expect nothing from this brilliant bubble blown by humanity;
I travel a land that exists; I can't bear the place, and I love it...

[GS]

The Choice
Mount Kisco

I too could have chosen to leave my home behind,
and be blissful or glum in a house with three bathrooms...
If I could have settled down to some decent profession...
I've even become a professor of sorts, more or less...
I'm only pushing this marble about, this twist of the rainbow –
the choice to stay Magyar was due to my hard business sense,
my nerves did their market-reseach, thoroughly Japanese.
The explosive mixture inherited from my parents
needed a steady hand and solid character,
only here in my home, the place I was born, could I be what I am,
here where whatever might happen, malarias of style could infect me,
the vice of misfortune and language would keep me in hand.
Poet, inventor. Like an Arizonian windsurfing in the desert,
I discovered my own piece of sky, flight through the dust.

[GS]

The Wide Horizon
FROM *Moby Dick*

Cowering in the the cellar of a narrow little country
I longed for a full panorama of circular vision,
the round mirror's convexity, its orbital compass –
I wasn't to know that there I'd end up squaring the circle...
The wide horizon (our smashed mouths tell us) is also a cross
that we're doomed to carry for ever from one hill to another –
each with his own and each in his manner...
The Cassandra of Greek myth and the sailor in the New Bedford dive
agree in their view of the public, which eyes them suspiciously:
We speak a different language, but use the same words...
Wisdom may serve as a medicine: nevertheless...I am aging;
instead of the bright panorama a well-focussed close-up
where ever more frequently the monster surfaces, white as a hospital,
and ploughs me under the waves, into dark water.

[GS]

The Snows of Yesteryear

Where is Mr Orbán, last year's visiting professor?
Where is his queer accent, his strange opinions?
Deep, deep, deep in the hill he sleeps,
like other citizens of the Spoon River.
I contemplate this man in boots and anorak,
whose grey curls peek out under his fur hat;
an aging party waiting for the bus to take him to St Paul –
I would not notice him were he not me...
Incredible that my past should belong to him,
still more incredible, that his is mine...
Some third person is writing my poems, one who knows my
            obsessions intimately,
before his eyes the orange malleable lava of the day before yesterday
is hardening to a dark basalt grey that one might study,
and the dumb snow falls like lint on the open wound of the world.

[GS]

The Flying Faust

By the time our spirits can fly our bodies are crippled –
something for something, state the terms of our contract,
which for the sake of precision we tied with the devil.
The Dread One, of course, is not a ringleted dandy wielding a
    trident,
nor a professor-cum-inspector of taxes thirsting for blood,
but an air-traffic controller with wider horizons than usual;
before our departure he strictly observes that we have surrendered
our childhood, our youth and our loves, our small sum of years
and in a syrupy baritone announces over the speaker:
'Tower to broom. Permission granted for take-off.'
And the world which is used to rubbishing its heroes, watches and
    cackles
as a pack of warty, twitching, wheezing grandads and grannies
straddle the broomstick and sing the loud praises
of all-renovating, flame-haired, eternal youth.

[GS]

A Visit to Room 104

I saw how death pursued its calling in peacetime;
carving fine detail, a vigilant minor craftsman:
one lump on the thighbone, one on the brain, one by the eyes –
he worked in fine temper and whistled a tune down the oxygen tube...
All our lives we prepare for the great Titus Dugovic scene
where we perform a spectacular double-twist dive off the castle
      ramparts
and make an impression on our descendants –
a downbeat ending comes as a surprise...
We're not prepared for the fact that our bodies pack up –
that we find no space in bed for our hands or our legs,
that we spend the whole night on a bed of sharp nails, tossing and
      turning...
mud then or spirit? The choice of the romantic,
of the archer with one eye shut, of the eschatologist –
from death's point of view all things are mud, even the spirit.

[GS]

The Exploded Treadmill

Should I trust in history, that elusive old harridan?
The past is idiotic and tells lies;
I was sitting by the bedside of my dying friend
smiling encouragement at him: everything's fine...
The present at least is certain. Certain intense schizophrenia –
in childhood I was an old man, now I long to recover
my mad adolescence as an ethical yardstick...
Sooner or later we grasp that our fickle companion for life, our talent
has rented its studio on that plot of land between bull and red rag,
and that patience in real life does not bear roses
but a heap of embers on the frame of a hospital bed...
There's nothing to trust in but my idle improvisations,
up to my neck in the grease, I pimple the world with a verse,
once in God's likeness, now a rattling and clattering old wreck...

[GS]

The Beauty of War

War's for the conquerors, for Alexander the Great,
the scoutmaster gazing with pleasure on his warriors warming
each other, stuck in life's freezer at that jamboree in Macedon.
They share their last fag, he brags to the Chronicle
though he heartily despises the liberal press
because they create such a stink at each piffling court-martial,
when even a blind man can see that civilisation's at stake...
What's done is done, always look on the bright side!
Alas, the barbed wire has a circular section, all sides are bright;
war is the thing that Pilinszky saw, at the age of twenty-four:
time spinning according to the law of the camera
a frozen frame from an accelerated film of mad alternatives,
a cage that preserves the glow of damnation, the smoke and the heat,
the victims like poultry waiting for slaughter, caught on the wire.

[GS]

Alban Berg: Opus 4, The Altenberg Songs

Schoenberg, Altenberg, Berg – a mountain-peak in all three names.
In other words our modern art is peaky.
So birdsong gives birth to dodecaphonics,
that logical cage in which there trills a canary with a diploma.
If you get to know the secrets of the trade, leave them at home,
work only from memory. The masterpiece is always accidental.
You need a slight touch of the dilettante
in order to believe in the sheeted ghost of absolute loneliness
which like a rusty hinge creaks at the door of the century...
Everything's against it, the fashion, Schoenberg himself;
in vain... In the jolly and bloody town of the king and the emperor
the elegant audience springs angrily to its feet to swat the composer –
forty more years before it learns what scrapes and billows like this,
what kind of wire glitters in the black smoke of damnation.

[GS]

The Father of the People

Which monarch-cum-deity had fewer restraints or more power?
His was the way, the truth and the life, but chiefly the death;
his world was as simple as Russian Roulette,
the red ball, obedience: the black, execution...
A brief generation, to see his fallen statues' living original –
the short-assed, vengeful, industrious genius of organisation,
who dickered with his penknife in a functioning watch,
because he failed to grasp the ideal in whose name he murdered.
Divinity requires a godlike imagination,
a pinch of poetry to go with the hard-line of strategy –
conscience and soul are not merely words in a spectrum,
sooner or later the lie starts to rot in the firm-looking binding,
and chronically sneezing, time, the monumental mason, carves on the
    tombstone
of common memory: Xerxes; Capone; the once fearful name of the
    emperor.

[GS]

Witchfinder General

In the imagined TV-series produced by neo-conservative ideology
Jean-Jacques Rousseau (quiet atmospheric music) goes for a walk
in the wood and finds a casket, opens it, and out flies the devil
who wears a new disguise each century, now Robespierre, now Hitler,
beats this vale of tears to a bloody pulp of millions of victims,
and with a blade honed on mass ideology trims beard and neck at
    once.
To be sure, by the time he gets home late at night, history is
    exhausted
and bored of the bloodbath at Vendée and Katyn Forest;
it longs for a bit of home cooking and TV in front of the fire...
The new fundamentalist of the age is a disappointed egghead,
a curved sabre forged on the anvil of elite universities in his hand,
while a sparkling inscription on the fine cutting edge of his wit
    reminds him
of the address and the postcode of hell: Paris, 1789.

[GS]

A Roman Considers the Christians

May the gods forgive me but I really can't abide them.
Their idea is a great one, but look at them all:
a bunch of quarrelsome eggheads picking their noses,
who, under the spell of their thesis, would if they could
be hard-line dictators, all for the sake of tolerance naturally,
who'd not kill with weapons but with murderous disdain,
while breeding their own sloppy aristocracy,
along with other oppressive, life-hating state institutions...
So, let me embellish this with a gesture – a fig for them all!
Just one little problem: the starved lion bawling in the arena...
There are plenty with vision, but they are the ones prepared to be
     eaten
in dust clouds of water-cannon, where out of the screaming and
     bloodshed
something emerges...the same thing? the worse? or the better?
the gods only know, if they know, what lies in the future...

[GS]

The Golem

The God of the tribe of the Jews makes a difficult partner;
his outline contract is all hard conditions: if, in so far as...
Did he create me? This dominant paterfamilias?
Or is he just the smoke coloured ghost of the war, prevalent
        conditions?
Whoever he was, he was old and forgetful,
he baked his figure of clay to the Kabbala recipe, but exhausted himself
so under the tongue of the creature he stuck the *shema*,
that piece of squared paper where he jotted down
what he was to do on the other days of that week,
and he can't remember what he then wrote nor where he put it...
As a child I was malleable, as an adult I turned to poetry,
a monster tottering stiffly towards some undefined target,
under my tongue glows my father's tatty inscription,
while I spit the millenium in small balls of paper back at the world.

[GS]

The Stranger's Perspective

'An outsider, if there were such a thing'
    – SZABOLCS VARADY

Unexpectedly glimpsing from the window of some interstellar
        spacecraft
that village brawl referred to as international conflict,
that little local flare-up of hot-blooded humanity,
the parties, insurrectionists, strident gesticulating soap-box orators,
the glowing nimbus of theories above droves of horny demons,
the road-tax, smoke-tax, tap-tax, air-tax, sky-tax and all other taxes,
the impalings, the racks, the burnings and the hangings,
in other words everything covered by the term East Central Europe,
and appreciating too that in this brothel where beggar screws beggar,
where, seeing the butterfly of tomorrow in the larva of today,
we're always trying to compose the golden section of freedom and
        plenty,
and that for some reason we're actually fond of our unbearable manias,
the angel of God, an unspoilt country bumpkin from an order of
        see-through angels,
is quite lost for words, his jaws hang open, mumbling:
        REALLY... REALLY...

[GS]